AGATHA CHRISTIE

HALLOWE'EN PARTY

BY CHANDRE

HARPER

Hello, family and friends!
And a big thank you to Manolo-Prolo for the advice — it worked!
Hello "Mrs Weasel"!
— Chandre

HARPER
An imprint of HarperCollins*Publishers*
77-85 Fulham Palace Road
Hammersmith, London W6 8JB
www.harpercollins.co.uk

First published by HARPER 2008
1

Comic book edition published in France as *Le Crime d'Halloween*
© Heupé SARL/Emmanuel Proust Éditions 2007
Based on *Hallowe'en Party* © 1969 by Agatha Christie Limited,
a Chorion Company. All rights reserved.
www.agathachristie.com

Adapted and illustrated by Chandre.
English edition edited by Harry Man.

ISBN 978-0-00-728054-4

Printed and bound in China.

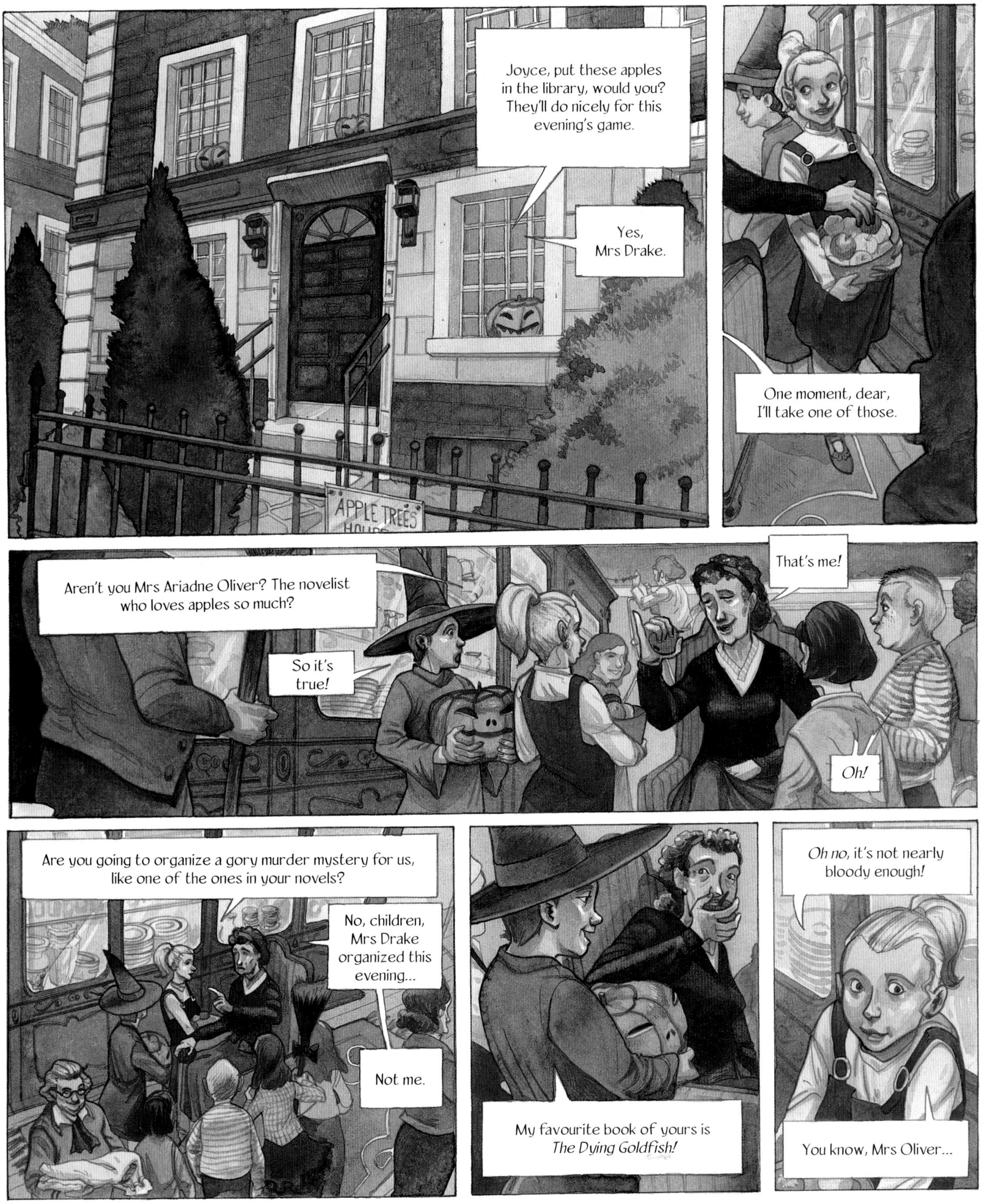
Joyce, put these apples in the library, would you? They'll do nicely for this evening's game.
Yes, Mrs Drake.
APPLE TREES
One moment, dear, I'll take one of those.
Aren't you Mrs Ariadne Oliver? The novelist who loves apples so much?
That's me!
So it's true!
Oh!
Are you going to organize a gory murder mystery for us, like one of the ones in your novels?
No, children, Mrs Drake organized this evening...
Not me.
My favourite book of yours is *The Dying Goldfish!*
Oh no, it's not nearly bloody enough!
You know, Mrs Oliver...

I witnessed a murder once, when I was little. I didn't understand what was going on at the time, but now...

Ah ha ha ha ha!

But it's true! I did! *I did!*

Nowadays the only thing that interests the young at parties is drink and drugs!

They're all hippies!

Ahem, ahem!

If could just get by...

Stupid old bag won't leave us alone.

Peace at last!

So many young people around and so much to do, it's exhausting!

Thank you for having us, Mrs Drake.

You're welcome. Thank you for not making a mess!

LONDON, HERCULE POIROT'S APARTMENT...

Rrring!

Hercule Poirot speaking.

Oh, Mrs Oliver, *mais bien sûr,* right away.

George, could you get me a cognac and a bitter lemon, and some apples, if you please.

Very good, sir.

We're expecting Mrs Oliver at any moment.

Brrring!

Oh! Here already!

Mrs Oliver, how lovely to see you again!

Oh, thank you, Poirot!

It's simply *dreadful!*

?

I don't know where to begin...

Why, at the beginning, my dear Ariadne.

Well, I've been staying with a dear friend, Judith Butler, at Woodleigh Common. They were organizing a Hallowe'en party for some teenagers...

We played for a while, then after supper it was time for a game of "snapdragon"...

You know, where you burn raisins in a great dish of brandy?

Then the parents came to pick up their children. Mrs Drake, the owner of the house, and the rest of us were just tidying up and...

and that's when we found her in the library.

Ariadne, who did you find?

The little girl. She'd been murdered — drowned in the apple-bobbing bucket!

When did this happen?

Last night.

Why didn't you come sooner?

To begin with, like everyone else, I was in shock from such a heinous crime. Joyce Reynolds was boasting and showing off.

But all the same, she didn't deserve what happened to her.

The more I think about it, the more something the little girl said that afternoon bothers me.

"I witnessed a murder once, when I was little. I didn't understand what was going on at the time..."

Woodleigh Common? It sounds familiar, where is it?

Near Medchester, about forty miles from London.

Any suspects?

The police think that it was two teenagers, but they don't have any proof. Besides us, there were 25 to 30 people there that day.

I'll handle this personally, we'll find the culprit.

For such a vile murder, there can be only one explanation: the murderer was at that party!

And my little grey cells are trying to tell me why Woodleigh Common is so familiar...

Bonjour, Superintendent Spence!

Good heavens! I know that moustache!

I see you're still growing it, Poirot!

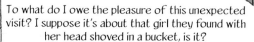

To what do I owe the pleasure of this unexpected visit? I suppose it's about that girl they found with her head shoved in a bucket, is it?

Précisément. I'm here on behalf of an author friend of mine.

Unfortunately, Poirot, I can't help you any more. I've retired from the police force.

That may be, but old habits die hard.

You know how it is — you were a police officer in Belgium.

You know the people around here, Spence — and you must have kept one eye open.

Yes, but Poirot, most people around here are just passing through for work.

Some even stay for a while...

But not long enough to want to murder someone.

I don't agree. The victim boasted that she had witnessed a murder when she was younger. That killer, overhearing this, hastened to cover his tracks once and for all!

Mrs Oliver thinks that there were about 15 people present at the moment of Mademoiselle Joyce's little outburst.

If you could help me build a precise list, that would be a great help...

Never fear, Poirot, I can help you. My sister Elspeth knows everyone in London!

I wouldn't expect anything less, *mon cher* Spence...

Just in time, Poirot!

Hardly the ideal location to commit a murder, *n'est-ce pas,* Ariadne?

After this, we'll go and see the mother of the victim, then the local chief inspector. My friend Spence is arranging it. I would also like to see Joyce's headmistress.

Ensuite, tea and sausages with Spence and his sister!

But you've spent the day with him — what more can he tell you?

Not him, his sister! She knows everyone!

You're like one of those computers... gathering all the bits of information and calculating the solution.

How do you do, I'm Mrs Drake. You must be Hercule Poirot?

The same. At your service, Madame

To have one's evening ruined is just ghastly don't you think Poirot, especially when a lunatic— of which there are so many these days — kills a child?

I'm convinced— that it's not that simple...

It seems quite plain to me that a mad man must have escaped the asylum and come looking for some vulnerable child.

The library...

That's where the bucket was.

We put it here during the game of snapdragon. The police took it...

When we found the body, her head was in the water and the carpet was damp. But everyone had got wet apple bobbing.

The victim is often the cause of the crime. Madame, what did you think of Joyce?

It doesn't bode well to speak ill of the dead, but Joyce was nothing more than a little liar.

She said she'd seen a murder. Of course, we all ignored her!

Bon, thank you for your help with those little details, Madame. I hope that it has not brought back too many unpleasant memories.

Forgive me, I do have one more question...

Have you heard anyone else talk about a murder in Woodleigh Common?

I do know that there were those two lorry drivers. A row broke out between them and a girl was found dead in the road with a rock in her hand. But Joyce would have been too young to remember that.

I think she made the story up to impress her friends and get the attention of Mrs Oliver.

!

Thank you, Mrs Drake.

Seems like a bad place to choose for murder...

She made it sound like it's my fault!

What's her husband like?

Oh, she's a widow, her husband died a couple of years ago. He was ill, suffered from polio for years.

He was run over by a car. He was dead the second it hit him. Unfortunately, nobody saw who the driver was.

So, no one took Joyce seriously? Not even the other children?

No, not even the children.

Mrs Drake would like to believe that the murder had never really happened, but I think she was pleased to be able to talk about it...

Ariadne, tell me something, do you like Mrs Drake?

She's bossy, likes running things. I don't much like bossy women.

And Joyce's mother, is she like that?

She's nice enough, but not very bright. It's pretty awful to have your daughter murdered, isn't it?

Yes, but you know how people think.

Mrs Reynolds must not blame herself.

Are you sure you want me to come with you to see her? She doesn't know me.

Bien sûr, I need you to help check that my calculations are correct.

?

Of course, the computer must stick to his programme!

Mrs Reynolds, do you have any idea who might have killed Joyce?

I dropped my children off at the party, I didn't go myself. It must have been someone from outside, some basket case — a man, I suppose. No woman could do a thing like that.

Are you aware that Joyce said she had once witnessed a murder?

What?!

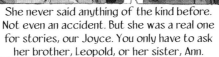

She never said anything of the kind before. Not even an accident. But she was a real one for stories, our Joyce. You only have to ask her brother, Leopold, or her sister, Ann.

Hello, Monsieur, that's an impressive plane. Tell me, did your sister ever see a murder?

Of course not! She liked to cause a fuss. All she wanted was Mrs Oliver's attention.

I heard her, but I didn't take any notice. There hasn't been a murder in Woodleigh Common for years!

Joyce was a compulsive liar. She did it to impress people, like the time she "went to India" with our uncle...

I am now convinced the mystery of Joyce's personality has been solved.

Like the boy who cried wolf, you mean?

She could well have seen something, but not a murder.

But she was killed!

And because of that we may never know the truth.

Okay, but what could she have seen?

Well, there are no easy answers, but there are some cases of interest that match the period and possibly the circumstances.

I've made you a small list.

First of all there's Mrs Llewellyn-Smythe, whose *au pair* disappeared within a fortnight of inheriting her employer's entire fortune...

Mrs Llewellyn-Smythe had a heart condition. Her death, although sudden, was not unexpected. She poured all her remaining energies into her garden.

She decided to get in contact with her nephew when she first became ill. She bought a nearby house, the one by the quarry. She fell in love with the thought of transforming the quarry into a sunk-garden and paid a landscape gardener, Michael Garfield, a fortune to plan it.

Mrs Llewellyn-Smythe was extremely wealthy. She had him construct a small house for himself in the grounds.

12

But her death was of natural causes, *non?*

Doctor Ferguson declared as much. However, the last will that she signed — a codicil — was found to be a forgery!

Her housekeeper admitted that Mrs Llewellyn-Smythe did not enjoy writing and put Olga Seminoff, the *au pair*, in charge of her correspondence.

Olga was asked if she'd written the codicil, but then she ran away.

Suppose Joyce overheard something that proved it was suspicious...?

Then how about Charlotte Benfield? Sixteen, a shop assistant, suffered head injuries, found dead near the quarry. Two suspects: Peter Gordon, 21, with a history of petty theft...

... and Thomas Hudd, 20, shy, used to stammer a lot, possibly mentally unstable. Both went out with Charlotte at some point. But Joyce Reynolds didn't live close to the quarry.

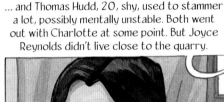

Hmm...

Unlikely. Any other murders Joyce could have seen?

Mr Lesley Ferrier? Lawyer's clerk, 28 years old, employed by Fullerton, Harrison and Leadbetter, Mrs Llewellyn-Smythe's solicitors. Stabbed in the back outside the Green Swan pub. He was having an affair with the landlord's wife.

The murder weapon was never recovered. Both the husband and the wife were suspected. They were jealous people and Lesley had a temper...

He'd been caught before falsifying his accounts.

Though he'd gone straight, he hung out with the wrong crowd.

A large sum of money was found in his account — deposited in cash. Nothing to show where it came from. That was suspicious in itself.

Again, not Joyce's murder, I don't think.

And Janet White?

Young teacher, found strangled on a footpath between the schoolhouse and her home.

That was two and a half years ago.

She shared a flat with another teacher, Nora Ambrose. She said Janet broke up with a young man who later resorted to sending her increasingly abusive letters, including death threats. Unfortunately, no trace of these letters was ever found.

Interesting...

Given the time it happened, it is possible that Joyce could have seen a struggle and misinterpreted it as an innocent game between two consenting adults. As she grew older, she realized he had been killing her!

Joyce made her announcement during the preparations for the party. Someone who heard her may have acted as soon as possible.

We can check the list of guests. But my dear Poirot, it's possible someone could have entered after the preparations and then left following Joyce's murder, so they won't be on it!

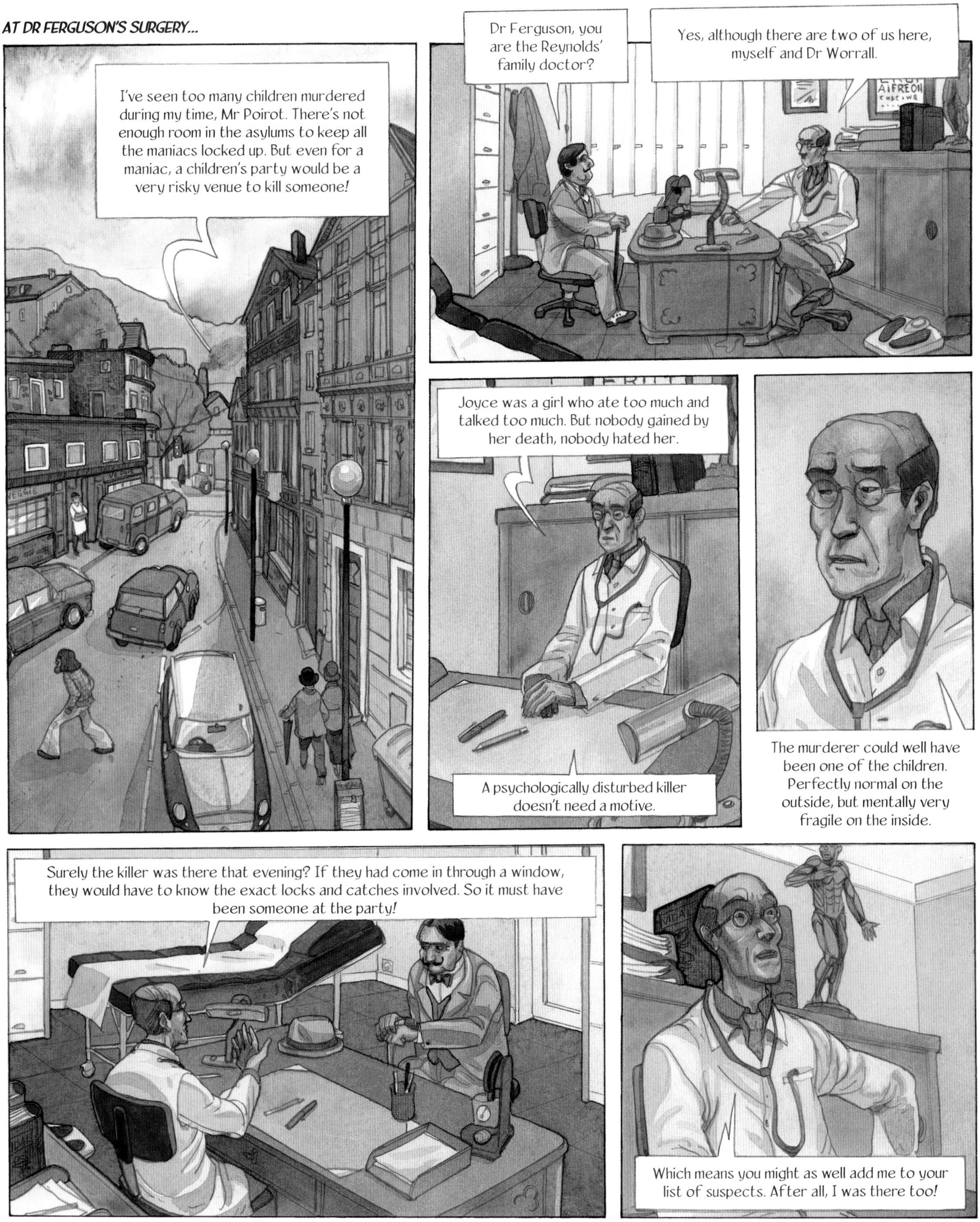
AT DR FERGUSON'S SURGERY...
I've seen too many children murdered during my time, Mr Poirot. There's not enough room in the asylums to keep all the maniacs locked up. But even for a maniac, a children's party would be a very risky venue to kill someone!
Dr Ferguson, you are the Reynolds' family doctor?
Yes, although there are two of us here, myself and Dr Worrall.
Joyce was a girl who ate too much and talked too much. But nobody gained by her death, nobody hated her.
A psychologically disturbed killer doesn't need a motive.
The murderer could well have been one of the children. Perfectly normal on the outside, but mentally very fragile on the inside.
Surely the killer was there that evening? If they had come in through a window, they would have to know the exact locks and catches involved. So it must have been someone at the party!
Which means you might as well add me to your list of suspects. After all, I was there too!

Mademoiselle Emlyn, as the headmistress of this school, would you say that you know every child in the village?

Yes, I know all the children of Woodleigh Common.

Mr Poirot, did you want to talk to me about Joyce Reynolds?

Somebody insane killed her. That's the only realistic explanation.

No, I'm not so certain, I am sure there was a motive: Joyce had been witness to a murder.

Joyce was a compulsive liar — she boasted to impress her friends.

I think she witnessed an accident or an injury and exaggerated the details.

We must assume that a murderer was at the Hallowe'en party.

Mademoiselle, do you remember the murder of Janet White, one of your staff?

Of course. It happened a couple of years ago. Beautiful girl, about 25 years old. She was killed while out walking alone. The police interrogated a few people, but no one ever found sufficient proof. A very sad state of affairs, both for her family and for the school...

You and I agree on the same principle: we do not approve of murder.

Yes, I like the way you put it. Now, I think you'd better speak to Mrs Whittaker. I'll go and get her.

Bonjour, Mademoiselle Whittaker. I was wondering if you could tell me if there were any unusual goings on during the preparations for the Hallowe'en party?

Hello, Mr Poirot.

Well, Mrs Drake was acting rather strangely...

I had just popped out of the room during a game of snapdragon when I caught sight of Mrs Drake on the landing. She was carrying a glass vase, but something seemed to startle her...

... because she dropped the vase, which smashed into smithereens.

What do you think startled her?

She was looking towards the door to the library. She might have seen something, maybe even someone.

Perhaps it was just the door handle moving, I don't know. Whatever it was gave her quite a fright and was not what she expected to see.

From where I was standing I couldn't really tell.

Then she composed herself and began picking up the pieces. I looked for a cloth to help her mop up. I asked her what had surprised her and she just said that it was nothing.

Madame Drake doesn't seem like the sort of person who startles easily.

No, but at the time I didn't ask myself that question. I had no idea that something terrible was about to happen, or had happened, to Joyce — that only came afterwards.

Do you remember how the evening started?

Just a few games: a broomstick competition, a balloon contest, a mirror of fortune game, and bobbing for apples...

Then was the flour and sixpence game, and we had supper and all played snapdragon.

I last saw Joyce at the flour and sixpence game.

So she must have died after this game.

Tell me, Mademoiselle, how long have you been a teacher?

Six years. I teach Latin and mathematics.

So you must remember Janet White? Joyce said that she had witnessed a murder. Perhaps it was that one? What can you tell me about Janet's relationship with Nora Ambrose?

They were both rather excitable, but in different ways...

What became of Nora Ambrose?

They were great friends. When Janet died, Nora was so upset that she upped sticks and moved north to teach there.

Thank you, Mademoiselle.

LATER...

STONE QUARRY HOUSE

C'est magnifique. I would love to meet Monsieur Garfield, what wonderful work.

This reminds me of Garinish Island in Ireland.

Why, speak of the devil!

Monsieur Garfield?

Is this private property?

It's not open to the public but people do walk here.

These days the place has a reputation for being rather unlucky after they found a dead body here a couple of years ago.

I sold both the house and gardens to the Westons after I inherited them from my former employer, Mrs Llewellyn-Smythe.

I congratulate you, these quarry gardens look stunning!

Thank you, but it is my job as gardener to make a place look as appealing as possible and so attract more clients.

You must be Hercule Poirot. I've heard a lot about you.

Your instincts are correct, that's me. Tell me, Monsieur Garfield, were you at the Hallowe'en party?

No, I wasn't.

And do you know the Reynolds family?

Of course, but I know most people in Woodleigh Common, by varying degrees of intimacy.

What did you think of Joyce Reynolds?

Not a great deal.

But then again I don't like children very much, Mr Poirot, they bore me.

I'm afraid I must take my leave of you, Monsieur Garfield.

I have a prior engagement, and I musn't be late.

Now, who's this...?

I expect you're Mr Hercule Poirot?

Yes!

I've come here to meet you. You are coming to tea, aren't you?

Come on, follow me...

And what's your name?

Miranda!

If we go this way, there's a shortcut.

It's my favourite place to go and walk.

There used to be an old fountain right in the middle there. It's all in bits and pieces now.

I like to hide in the shrubs and the trees and watch the birds and squirrels. Hardly anyone comes this way.

Everyone's scared of this garden because somebody was killed here.

Joyce was my best friend, Mr Poirot. We shared all of kinds of secrets, like the time when she rode on the back of that elephant in India.

I know Joyce was drowned in a bucket of water. Mum didn't want to tell me. Mrs Perring the cook told me in the end.

I wasn't at the party, I was too unwell... follow me!

It's a secret passage!

It's not the easiest passage, *mon dieu!*

Aren't you glad you didn't have to walk all that way?

Miranda! Did you make poor Mr Poirot come through the hedge?

Allow me to introduce you to my friend, Judith Butler.

Enchanté.

How do you do, Mr Poirot.

This whole affair makes me think of that quote, who was it, Walter Scott or Burns: "There is a child among you taking notes."

It's perhaps best not to take every word Joyce said as gospel, especially a matter so serious as murder.

After all, she never talked about it.

It seems everyone in Woodleigh Common would have me believe that Joyce was a compulsive liar.

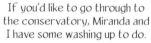

If you'd like to go through to the conservatory, Miranda and I have some washing up to do.

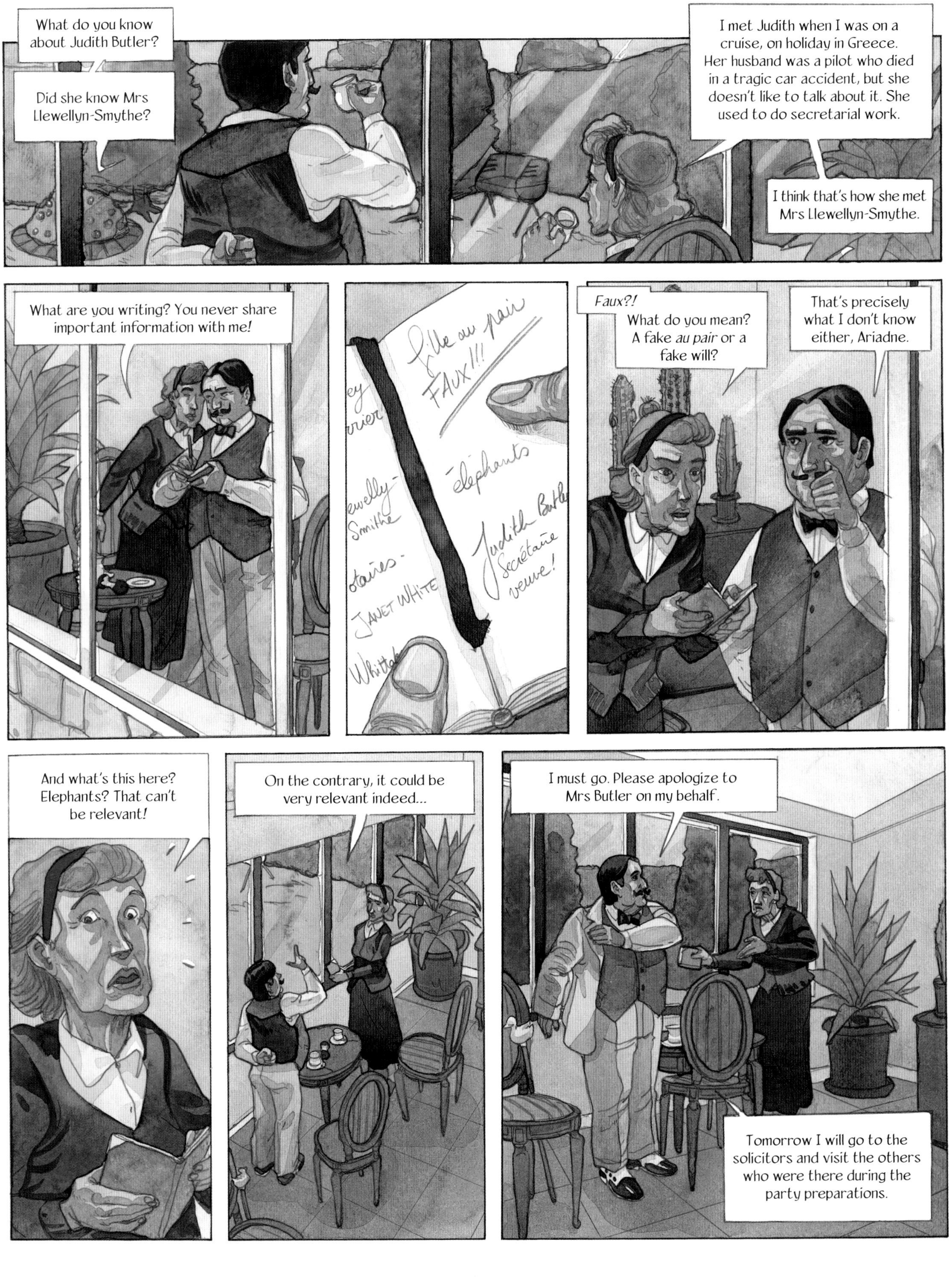
What do you know about Judith Butler?
Did she know Mrs Llewellyn-Smythe?
I met Judith when I was on a cruise, on holiday in Greece. Her husband was a pilot who died in a tragic car accident, but she doesn't like to talk about it. She used to do secretarial work.
I think that's how she met Mrs Llewellyn-Smythe.
What are you writing? You never share important information with me!
fille au pair FAUX!!!
elephants
Judith Butler Secrétaire veuve!
JANET WHITE
Faux?!
What do you mean? A fake au pair or a fake will?
That's precisely what I don't know either, Ariadne.
And what's this here? Elephants? That can't be relevant!
On the contrary, it could be very relevant indeed...
I must go. Please apologize to Mrs Butler on my behalf.
Tomorrow I will go to the solicitors and visit the others who were there during the party preparations.

Mr Fullerton, you were Mrs Drake's solicitor, were you not? Is that how you met Mrs Llewellyn-Smythe?

Yes, that's right.

Was there anything suspicious about the death of Mrs Llewellyn-Smythe?

No, it was just one of those things...

And the death of Lesley Ferrier? That was a crime of passion, no?

No, I don't think so. While he was working for us he developed a bad reputation, and that could have had just as much to do with his violent death.

Do you think anyone might have witnessed his murder?

A child for example?

Why are you so interested in Lesley Ferrier's murder? It's not like it happened the other day.

Joyce said before she was murdered that she had been witness to a crime. Knowledge of such events therefore is most important.

All the same, it seems rather peculiar to be so interested in events that are so far back in the past.

There has also been a disappearance, has there not? A young *au pair* girl?

Olga Seminoff. She was helping Mrs Llewellyn-Smythe around the house. The lady was most grateful for her services.

Few people here would disagree.

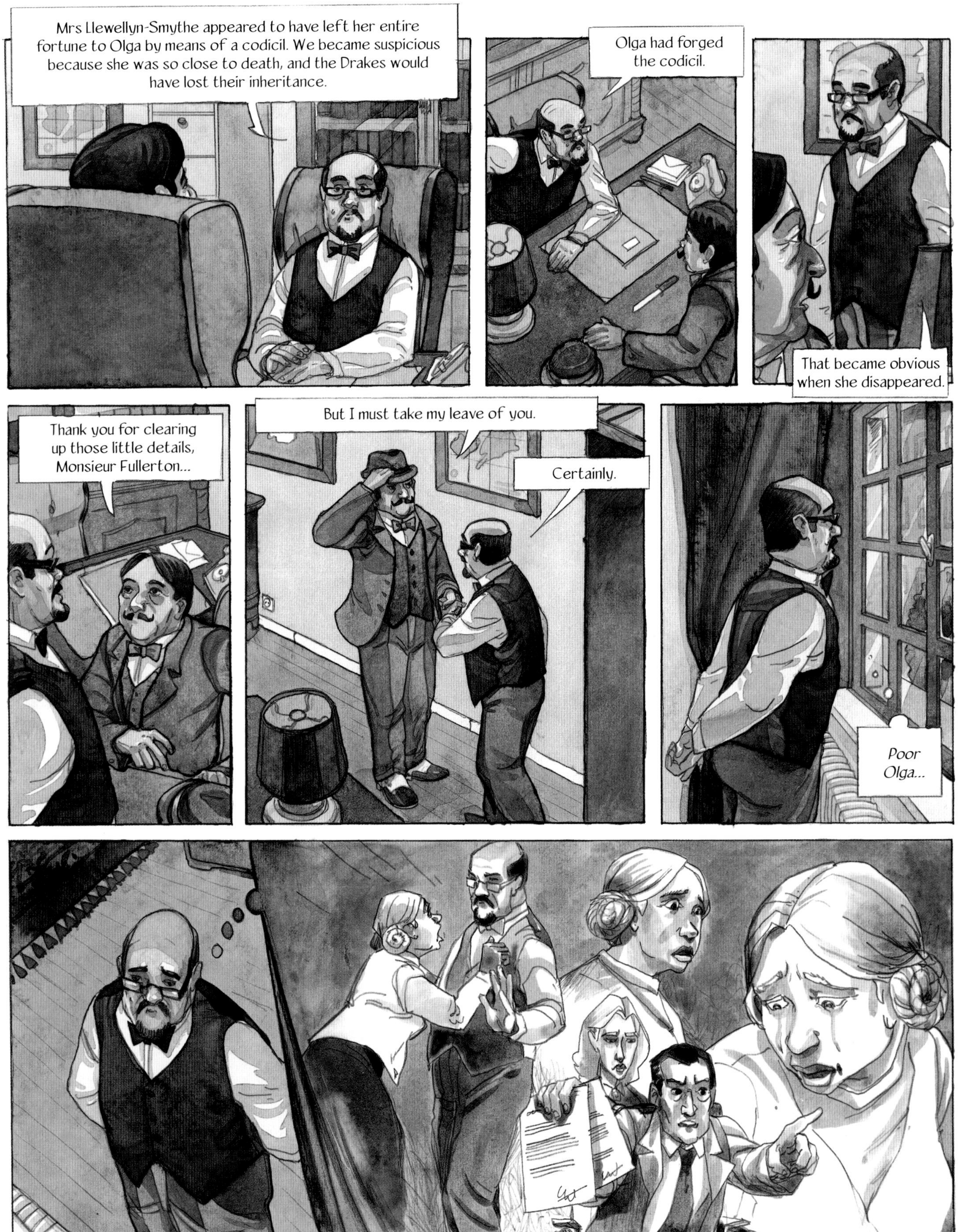
Mrs Llewellyn-Smythe appeared to have left her entire fortune to Olga by means of a codicil. We became suspicious because she was so close to death, and the Drakes would have lost their inheritance.
Olga had forged the codicil.
That became obvious when she disappeared.
Thank you for clearing up those little details, Monsieur Fullerton...
But I must take my leave of you.
Certainly.
Poor Olga...

Monsieur Poirot! I'm sorry to keep you waiting.

Bonjour, Madame Drake.

Could I ask you to help me with something that happened that night? Mrs Whittaker informs me that you seemed startled on the night of the murder.

And that you let go of the vase which you were holding and let it crash to the floor.

It was too heavy, I'd filled it up with water.

You did not see something unexpected in the doorway leading to the library?

No, I didn't see anyone.

That is most reassuring.

Perhaps Mrs Whittaker is the one who saw something and now she is trying to protect someone she knows, perhaps even one of her own pupils?

Do you think the killer was someone at the party? A teenager perhaps?

Why not? The young today are so aggressive. They vandalise everything in their path, so why wouldn't they carry out a murder?

Am I correct that you share the point of view of the police that it was a young person?

How could it not be? I have the utmost respect for the police. They're extremely efficient and capable, even if they couldn't find the monster that killed my husband.

In a hit and run it's difficult to find any proof, Mrs Drake.

Was that before or after your aunt's death?

A little bit after. He was crossing the road when a car came hurtling down the street. Confined to his wheelchair he was unable to get out of the way. The driver just kept going. It was a teenager, there's no doubt about it.

People like that ought to be found and put away for good!

But my husband was not killed on purpose, not like Joyce.

So you think she was murdered for a reason?

Joyce was nothing but a little liar.

So many people have told me that, I might just start believing them!

Nobody would know Joyce's character better than Miss Whittaker and Miss Emlyn. The two of them know all the children in Woodleigh.

I would prefer it if you could tell me a little bit more about someone else, Olga Seminoff. She was in the service of your aunt, no?

You've done your homework! Yes, she was. She was the one who tried to swindle my aunt. She made friends with a young solicitor in Medchester.

Goodbye, Mr Poirot.

Au revoir, Madame.

Nice bloke that Mr Drake, you know...

What can you tell me about the circumstances of the accident?

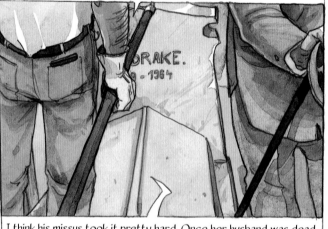

Two bearded fellas. They didn't stop, that's what they say. They found the car later, abandoned...

DRAKE.
9 - 1964

I think his missus took it pretty hard. Once her husband was dead she didn't have much left to live for. She kept busy, mind you.

She did everything for him. No wonder she went abroad for such a long time after.

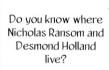

Do you know where Nicholas Ransom and Desmond Holland live?

Third house on the left, they live with Mrs Brand.

Do you think they're the ones what did it?

No, but they're part of the list of people who were there...

And I'm running out of people on my list...

28

I don't see how we can be any more help. We've already been interviewed twice by the police!

Well you were there during the preparations that evening and your testimonies were of great interest...

Basically we were just putting up fairy lights.

We put together the stuff for the mirror of fortune game.

We had some wicked disguises!

Tell me, any ideas on who might be the murderer? Perhaps you saw something?

I was hoping you could provide some clues?

I'm glad you asked.

Miss Whittaker is a really peculiar old spinster!

Don't you reckon? And you remember that other teacher who got strangled?

What? Maybe she did her in too?

Why not? Spending all morning at Apple Trees House is enough to drive anyone barmy.

Exactly, and she could have overheard Joyce!

So she snaps and kills Joyce to protect herself. Miss Emlyn then covers for her to protect the kids in her class!

What about the vicar? Sent off his rocker by all the hellfire and baptismal water of the snapdragon game!

Yeah, or something about sex, it's usually about that...

Thank you, gentlemen, for your elaborate deductions. You've certainly given me plenty to think about!

You know, Mr Poirot, I was having a wonderful time that evening.

Mrs Drake borrowed my witch's ball for the party, *hee hee!*

And what have you seen in it, Madame Goodbody?

Be careful what you wish for...

Do you know the devil's children, Mr Poirot? They are the worst, the ones who look like angels yet do the most awful things without conscience.

Yes, yes, I'm sure Joyce was a compulsive liar!

Odd things crop up in families. You take the Reynolds, for example. Leopold is a cunning little one who hides his tricks.

He is a clever soul but with bad intentions. Where does the money come from for all his gadgets?

Not his mother, that's for sure.

Thank you for your help, Madame Goodbody, you have been most insightful. Before I go, what can you tell me about Olga Seminoff?

Didn't go far. "*Ding dong dell, pussy's in the well.*" That's what I think.

Hello, you must be Mrs Oliver?

Yes, can I help you?

I'm Mrs Leaman, I'm here because I know something about Joyce's murder that might interest you.

Oh!

I was a cleaner working for Mrs Llewellyn-Smythe. I was called in to her study to sign a paper concerning Olga Seminoff.

There was another witness, James Jenkins, the gardener. He lives in Australia now.

After we'd finished, we left the door slightly open. Through the gap I saw her tuck the paper into a book. The next day I read it — the paper was a codicil leaving her fortune to Olga.

So the document was legal.

Olga was often a bit sharp, but she was always polite with Mrs Llewellyn-Smythe.

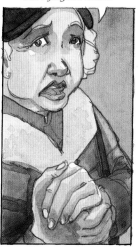

When it was declared a forgery, I didn't want to say anything, but it's been worrying me since.

The death of Mrs Llewellyn-Smythe wasn't that unexpected, but now that little girl's been murdered... Maybe Joyce saw someone put something in her tea?

Olga could have killed Mrs Llewellyn-Smythe to get her inheritance. Maybe that's what Joyce saw?

I've got to go now, so long.

31

You're not eating apples?

No, not since Joyce's murder, I've been completely put off them!

I'm eating Tunis dates.

Help yourself, they're delicious.

Ah, Poirot, I have something that you might be surprised to hear!

Ah, dates! But of course!

The dates must match!

Dates?

Yes, dates, as in calendar dates! Olga was accused of forgery. Lesley, the young solicitor, was caught for fraud. But it's not so simple...

It all hinges upon the dates!

Are you going back to London, Ariadne?

The day after tomorrow. Why?

Could you have someone over to stay in your house?

How well do you know Mrs Butler?

Someone who could be being threatened, whose life might very well be in danger!

I wouldn't say we're close friends. Miranda and Judith could be characters from one of my books. You don't need to know someone well to turn them into characters in a novel!

Are they the ones I would be having to stay?

Not until I am sure that one of my little ideas might be right.

You and your little ideas! Well, I have a snippet of information for you: the codicil was not a forgery!

So it was real! But how do you know that?

Through Mrs Leaman. You crossed paths as you arrived. She and a certain James Jenkins, Mrs Llewellyn-Smythe's gardener, were witnesses and had to sign it!

Could I use your telephone?

I don't think that Mrs Butler will have any objections.

Monsieur Fullerton?

Now that is strange! Jenkins did co-sign the codicil, but it wasn't witnessed by Harriet Leaman but by Mary Doherty, now deceased.

There must be two codicils, one real and one fake. Why would Mrs Leaman lie to me?.

Go on, Ariadne...

I want to know more about Olga Seminoff and why she fled!

Don't worry, chère Ariadne, we will know more about this as soon as I get information from my contact in Herzogovinia.

And the strangled teacher?

Have you spoken to Mrs Whittaker? I wouldn't be surprised if she was involved.

Absolutely, your little grey cells serve you well!

Exquisite, Monsieur Garfield!

Why, Poirot!

Thank you, but it's just a souvenir. When I leave, no one will be able to keep the place as wild as it is now...

You're leaving?

Yes, soon.

Has Miranda come here to be sketched by you?

No, she turned up. She's looking for a wishing well.

Hello, Mr Poirot!

A well?

Yes, it was here even before the place was just a quarry.

Michael knows where it is but he won't tell me!

It's more fun if you have to search for it. And it may not even exist!

It's hidden around here somewhere. Mrs Goodbody told me that to make a wish you must walk backwards around the well three times. But it was broken up because it was too dangerous. A child fell down it a long time ago.

Goodbye, Michael!

Bye, Mr Poirot!

Good luck!

Tell me, Monsieur Garfield, was there really a wishing well here?

Sort of. There is a well, and there was a wishing tree.

So why are you leaving?

I am leaving because my services are in demand, I'm doing a garden for Mrs Drake. The trouble is, so many of these people don't understand gardens and have no taste.

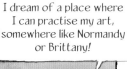

I dream of a place where I can practise my art, somewhere like Normandy or Brittany!

Perhaps a Greek island?

Do you know a Lesley Ferrier?

Yes.

He was the clerk who was stabbed. He was a womanizer, only interested in as many conquests as possible, and not just English women, foreigners too. He was fooling around with Olga Seminoff in secret. Mrs Llewellyn-Smythe didn't know anything about it...

His affair upset the other girls.

Olga could have lost her nerve over the forgery they put together, and so she cleared off, hoping Lesley would carry the can for it!

Hmm... fascinating.

A dishonest clerk and a philanderer!

I see where you're coming from. You're drawing connections between the two.

Why do you come to my wood to talk to me about these things?

You want beauty at any price, Monsieur Garfield...

For me, it is truth I want. Always truth.

Go on home to your police friends and leave me here in my local paradise.

Get thee away, Satan!

Ah, Poirot, there you are! My brother is down at the station. Something's happened but I don't know what.

This letter came for you.

Thank you, Mademoiselle McKay!

Monsieur Goby's foreign service always brings results! So, Olga Seminoff did not return to her home country but spoke of an impending marriage in a letter to a friend.

Mr Poirot! I must speak with you urgently! Come quickly! There's been another murder...

Her brother — Leopold Reynolds!

What?!

He was found on the way to school, drowned in a brook!

I wanted to tell you something before...

Tell me what, Mrs Drake?

When you came to see me to ask me about the party and why I was startled and why I dropped the vase. I lied to you!

I did see someone trying to leave the library.

It was Leopold!

36

I learned that Leopold had been very flush with money recently. After what has happened, I think the killer must have being paying him to keep his mouth shut.

I must go immediately! It's imperative that I see some people as soon as possible!

First of all I thought that he might have been the killer. I didn't say anything because I wanted to protect him — he's only a child! But now that he's dead, I must come clean. He must have just come from seeing his dead sister!

Now, Mademoiselle Emlyn...

TAXI

"ELMTREES" School

I've written four words on this paper...

I will ask you if you agree with them.

As to two of the words on that paper, I agree, yes. The other two, that is more difficult.

Parfait! We have had the same reaction!

Hercule Poirot has solved the mystery!

Leopold died because he became too greedy...

Now the assassin is more dangerous than ever because the only way out is to murder someone!

Before I go, I have one last question: are Nicholas Ransom and Desmond Holland trustworthy people?

Yes.

THE NEXT DAY...

Telegram for Mrs Oliver!

Quick, Judith! Pack your bags! Poirot has asked me to take you and Miranda to London!

But...!

I'm just going to say goodbye to a friend!

Miranda, we're going right now!

Who are Miranda's friends?

The only real friend I knew of was Joyce. They used to share stories about tigers and elephants.

Mum, can I leave Cathie a message first?

Yes, but be quick!

I'm coming!

You seem quite sure, Mr Poirot.

Yes, we cannot afford to waste any time now that we have proof.

"Ding dong dell, pussy's in the well."

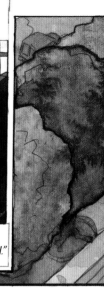

There are not many reasons a girl disappears. The first is that she has gone away with a man. The second is that she is dead.

My men are carrying out your excavation.

Anything else, Poirot?

Indeed. I have been in touch with a well-known firm of estate agents, friends of mine who specialize in real estate in the Mediterranean...

Here is a recent purchase that might interest you. I have an eye-witness on her way to London now. Even though I have taken every precaution possible, I am concerned for her. We are facing ruthlessness, greed pushed beyond limit, and perhaps even a touch, shall we say, of madness?

And madness can grow and take over very quickly!

RESCO ROAD

39

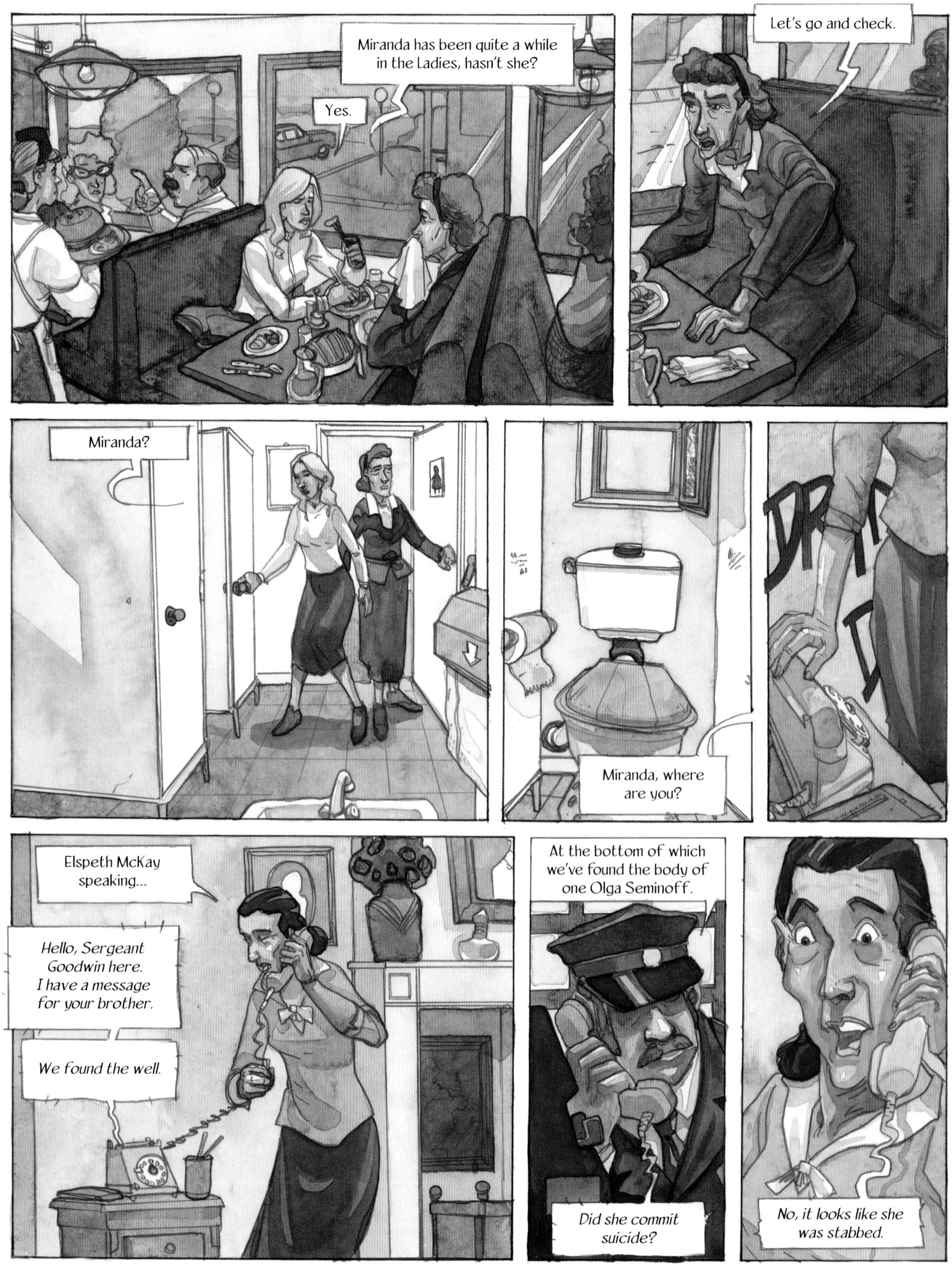
Miranda has been quite a while in the Ladies, hasn't she?
Yes.
Let's go and check.
Miranda?
Miranda, where are you?
Elspeth McKay speaking...
Hello, Sergeant Goodwin here. I have a message for your brother.
We found the well.
At the bottom of which we've found the body of one Olga Seminoff.
Did she commit suicide?
No, it looks like she was stabbed.

You look funny disguised like that!

You can laugh all you want... you'll see the double axe as it ought to be seen. And Kilterbury Down, too. Wonderful view.

You're right, it's amazing!

You idiots!

Don't you think Mum will worry about me?

POIROT'S APARTMENT...

Rrring!

Poirot speaking...

It's Ariadne. We've lost Miranda!

How did that happen?

In a restaurant. She didn't come back from going to the loo.

Somebody saw her leave with an old man, but they can't be sure!

Tell the police, say it's urgent! She's in great danger! We've found the body...

Body? What body?

Olga Seminoff, at the bottom of the well!

41

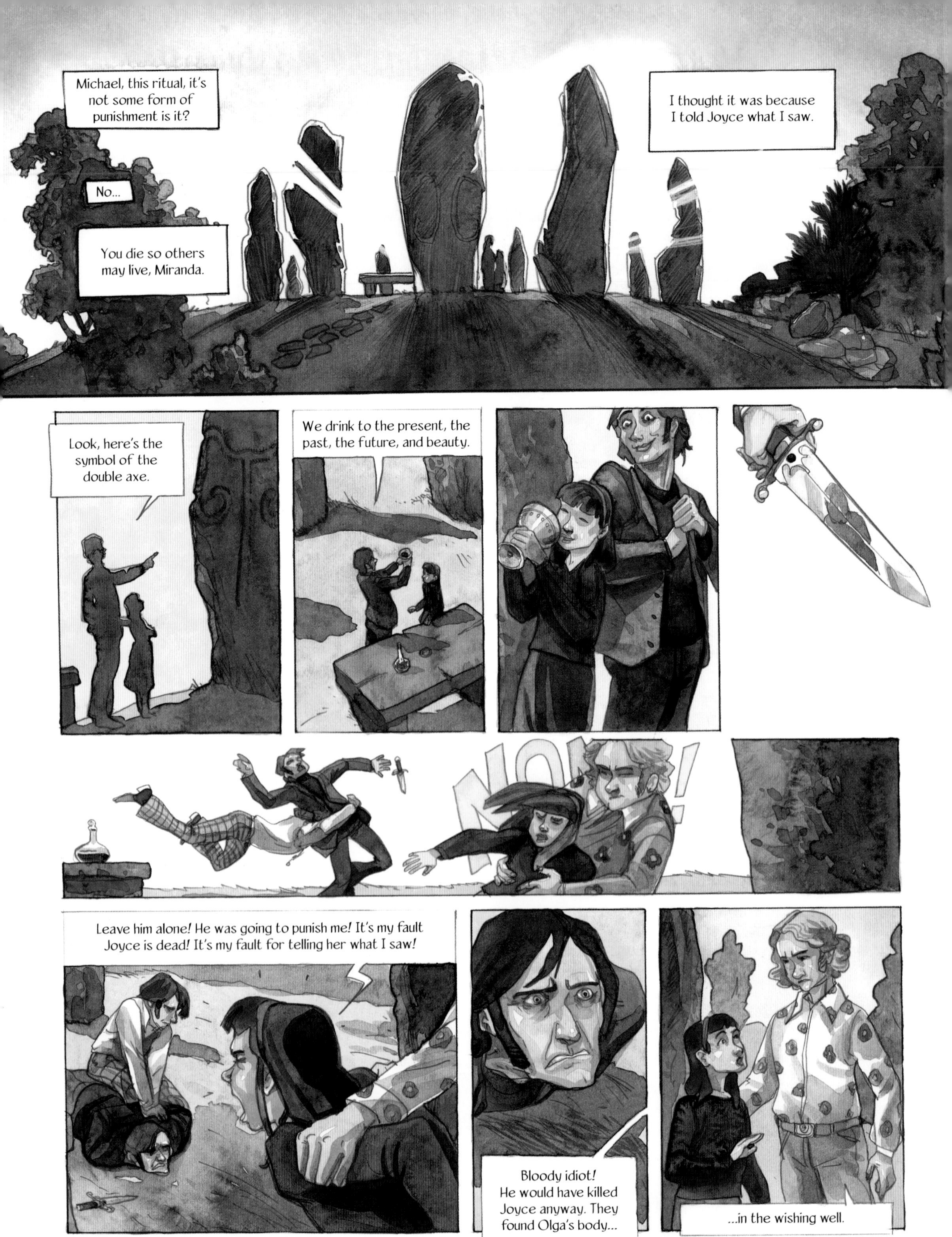
Michael, this ritual, it's not some form of punishment is it?
No...
You die so others may live, Miranda.
I thought it was because I told Joyce what I saw.
Look, here's the symbol of the double axe.
We drink to the present, the past, the future, and beauty.
NON!
Leave him alone! He was going to punish me! It's my fault Joyce is dead! It's my fault for telling her what I saw!
Bloody idiot! He would have killed Joyce anyway. They found Olga's body...
...in the wishing well.

Inspector Raglan, Superintendents Spence and Paddy, may I introduce you to Miranda and Judith Butler, and this is Desmond Holland and Nicholas Ransom.

Alors, Miranda, what did you see two years ago that you later told Joyce?

I was playing in the woods, watching all the squirrels, when I saw two people. They were carrying a body.

To begin with I just thought someone had fallen from somewhere. The next day I didn't think anything of it.

Then a few months later when I saw the two of them again, they were saying something about a Greek island, something like *"It's all sewn up, we can go whenever we want."*

Then I think I was spotted because she said, *"Shh... shut up, I think someone's watching us!"* That's when I knew what I'd seen had to have been a murder.

When I told Joyce about what happened, I think Leopold overheard....

Why didn't you say anything?

I was quite scared! Michael told me it had been a sacrifice and that it was necessary so that good life could keep on going.

Tell us, Miranda, who were the two people that you saw?

They were Michael Garfield and Mrs Drake.

43

Poirot, how did you know that Rowena Drake was Joyce's killer?

One vital clue: water.

Water?

It occurred to me that whoever drowned Joyce must have been very wet...

No one who forcibly drowns a child could do it without getting soaked.

Joyce had no suspicion of Madame Drake. Miranda had not told her who the murderers were.

All Madame Drake had to do was to wait with her vase at the top of the stairs until there was a witness. Madame Whittaker saw her...

... and she dropped the vase to give herself an alibi for being wet. That was her mistake, and that's what Miss Emlyn had also grasped when I spoke to her.

But how did you know it was Miranda who had been the original witness?

Everyone did their best to tell me Joyce was a liar. But she and Miranda told each other all their secrets...

It became the only plausible conclusion when your daughter said she always went to the woods. Woods which were home to at least one murder!

As for Michael, he wanted money to exercise his creative urges. When Monsieur Drake died, it was Madame Drake who became the sole inheritor. So Michael established a relationship with her.

Only Mrs Lewellyn-Smythe found out, and, in a fit of rage, cut Madame Drake from her will, leaving her fortune to Olga Seminoff.

Michael said Olga was in a relationship with Lesley Ferrier, which was not true. On the contrary, Michael was the one who paid Ferrier to falsify the codicil before making him disappear.

That codicil was a forgery, so Mrs Drake once again became the sole inheritor. All he had to do was to dispose of her.

Olga was then accused of forgery and her disappearance seemed to confirm her guilt.

Michael killed Olga and threw her down the well. The knife we found corresponded to the wounds found in the body of Lesley Ferrier.

It was Mrs Goodbody who pointed me in the direction of the well. Miranda told me Michael knew where it was.

Find the well, then find the proof!

I knew I was right when I heard him slip up in the throes of madness: *"Get thee away, Satan!"*

It should be "Get thee behind me..." For him, his work was sacred..

Miranda was the true witness. After having killed Leopold, he would now have to dispose of her.

They were sufficiently close that she would telephone him if she was going anywhere...

Between ourselves, Madame Butler...

is Michael Garfield Miranda's father?

What?!

There's no hiding from you, is there, Mr Poirot?

I knew Michael well before moving here. When I became pregnant, I left him. He never knew about it.

Soon afterwards I changed my name.

Good heavens!

When he came to the village for work, he didn't remember who I was.

How did you know?

Watching Michael and Miranda, there were some similarities in appearance, some physical traits.

Without knowing it, Garfield would have sacrificed his own daughter!

Mrs Drake will probably be locked away for the rest of her days...

While he was a victim of his own madness...

...on the point of surrender, he seized the poisoned goblet and saw his life run off from his body, like the last trickle of poison into the grass, all in the name of beauty...

CHRISTIE

CHANDRE07

CHAMONIX, le 11 août 2007

THE END